Thanksgiving Crafts

Thanksgiving Crafts

★ A Holiday Craft Book ★

★ Judith Hoffman Corwin ★

FRANKLIN WATTS

New York ★ Chicago ★ London ★ Toronto ★ Sydney

★ **Also by Judith Hoffman Corwin** ★

African Crafts
Asian Crafts
Latin American and Caribbean Crafts

Colonial American Crafts: The Home
Colonial American Crafts: The School
Colonial American Crafts: The Village

Easter Crafts
Halloween Crafts
Valentine Crafts
Kwanzaa Crafts

Papercrafts

Forthcoming Books

Christmas Crafts
Hanukkah

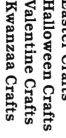

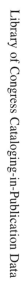
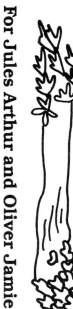

★ **For Jules Arthur and Oliver Jamie** ★

Library of Congress Cataloging-in-Publication Data

Corwin, Judith Hoffman.
  Thanksgiving crafts / Judith Hoffman Corwin.
    p.   cm. — (Holiday crafts)
  Includes index.
  ISBN 0-531-11147-4
  1. Thanksgiving decorations—Juvenile literature.   2.
Juvenile literature.   3. Thanksgiving cookery—Juvenile literature.
[1. Thanksgiving decorations.   2. Handicraft.   3. Thanksgiving
cookery.]   I. Title.   II. Series: Corwin, Judith Hoffman.   Holiday
crafts.
  TT900.T5C668   1995
  745.594'1—dc20
                                                    93-6369
                                                     CIP
                                                      AC

Contents

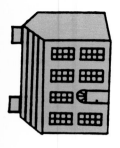

About Thanksgiving

A thanksgiving festival at harvest time has roots deep in ancient customs. Since people first harvested crops, there have been harvest festivals. The ancient Greek goddess Demeter, goddess of plant life and farming, was honored with a harvest festival. Her daughter, Persephone, was the goddess of the seasons. The ancient Romans held a festival called Ceralia in the autumn to honor their goddess of the harvest, Ceres. Our word *cereal* comes from her name.

The ancient Hebrews celebrated two harvest festivals 3,000 years ago. One, called Shavuoth, was held in the spring, when the figs were harvested. Another Jewish harvest festival, Sukkoth, is held in the autumn. A sukkah, or small booth decorated with leaves, branches, fruits, and nuts, is built and special prayers are said inside it.

The ancient Egyptians held a harvest festival in honor of Min, the god that they believed made their land fertile. The first sheaf of grain was cut by the Pharaoh, or ruler. The Pharaoh was thought to be a god also, so this act was to bring plenty in future harvests.

A harvest festival called Hung-Ch'iu was held in ancient China. It was the birthday of the moon, or queen of the night, and was celebrated when the moon was brightest, on the fifteenth day of the eighth month. It was a harvest moon.

Traditions, customs, folklore, and symbols have come down to us from these ancient celebrations. The harvest moon; the cornucopia or horn of plenty overflowing with fruits, nuts, vegetables, and flowers; the turkey dinner, groups of Pilgrims and Native Americans sharing a feast; cornstalks, ears of multicolored Indian corn—all of these are symbols of Thanksgiving Day. Gratitude for abundance is at the heart of today's thanksgiving feast, just as it was at those early harvest festivals.

Our American Thanksgiving was first celebrated in 1621 at the Plymouth Colony in Massachusetts. Governor William Bradford ordered a day of thanksgiving for having survived the very hard times the new settlers had faced. All the colonists and the Native Americans of the area shared this great feast together. The Native Americans had helped the early colonists, showing them new and wonderful foods so they would not starve. The Native Americans taught the settlers to gather cranberries, to plant corn, to hunt wild turkeys, and to dig for clams.

After the American Revolution, President George Washington proclaimed the first national Thanksgiving Day to honor the adoption of the United States Constitution. This first American Thanksgiving was held on November 26, 1789. After that, days of thanksgiving were held in various parts of our country at different times. After the victory at Gettysburg in 1863, Abraham Lincoln named the last Thursday in November as Thanksgiving Day. However, Thanksgiving was not fully established as a national holiday. Each state could decide when its Thanksgiving Day would be held. Finally, in 1941, when Franklin D. Roosevelt was president, Congress passed a special resolution declaring that Thanksgiving was to be celebrated on the fourth Thursday of November.

Thanksgiving is a time to get together with family and friends. It's a time to think about all that we have, and think, too, about how we can make the world an even better place than it is. Thanksgiving is a time to say thank you and to share our abundance with others who are less fortunate.

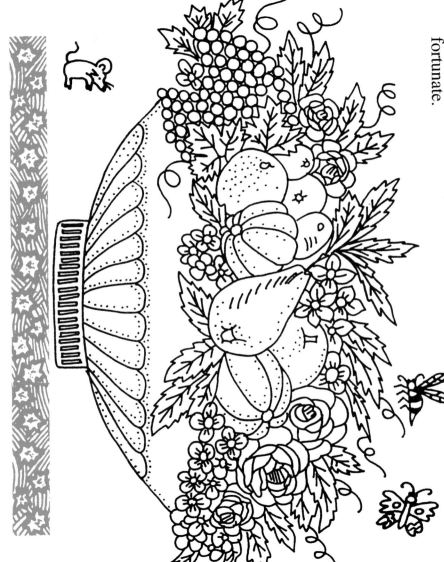

Let's Get Started

This book will help you find out about the Thanksgiving holiday, its legends and history. It is full of ideas for making decorations, presents, and wonderful treats to eat to celebrate the holiday. Often you will be able to make everything yourself, from everyday household supplies and objects. Use your imagination and you will be surprised at what you can create. The treasures you make will add color and excitement to your celebration.

Directions for many of the projects include patterns for you to use to make a copy of what is shown. You don't want to cut up this book, so copy the pattern with tracing paper. Begin by placing a piece of tracing paper over the pattern to be copied from the book. Using a pencil with a soft lead, trace the outline of what is in the book. Turn the paper over and rub all over the pattern with the pencil. Turn it over again, and tape or hold it down carefully on the paper or fabric you have chosen to work with. Draw over your original lines, pressing hard on the pencil. Then lift up the tracing-paper pattern and go on with the other instructions for your project.

A Bounty of Graces

Here are two prayers of thanksgiving that you might want to share with your family and friends at Thanksgiving dinner. The first one is by a famous American poet, the second one I wrote. Maybe you can think of one of your own and write it down. You might include it on your pop-up turkey invitation or on a greeting card.

For each new
morning with its light,
For rest and shelter
of the night,
For health and food,
for love and friends,
For everything Thy
goodness sends.

Ralph Waldo Emerson

We give thanks for our daily bread—
for this plentiful harvest.
For the blessings of the land, the waters, and the air.
Let your spirit go forth to renew the face of the earth
and show your love and kindness in the earth's bounty.
Save us from the selfish use of your gifts.
Grant that we who are filled with good things from your hand,
may never close our hearts to the hungry, the homeless, or the needy.

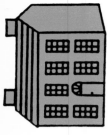

Cornucopia

The cornucopia, or horn of plenty, is a symbol of the fruits of the harvest for which thanksgiving is offered. It is usually shown overflowing with fruits, vegetables, nuts, and flowers. Corn and wheat are always included in the picture because they are used to make bread—a basic food of our diet.

Since ancient times the cornucopia has been a symbol of the earth's bounty. One ancient Greek myth tells of a goat named Amalthaea who nursed the god Zeus when he was a baby. Once Amalthaea broke off one of her horns and filled it with fruits and flowers for Zeus. Zeus placed an image of the goat in the sky as the constellation called Capricorn. In another myth, Zeus made Amalthaea's horn the horn of plenty that was to supply an abundance of whatever she wanted. You can draw your own cornucopia and use it as a holiday decoration. Follow the directions on page 9 and copy this design onto a piece of white paper. Color it in, using bright autumn colors.

Native American Designs

For centuries before the arrival of European settlers, Native Americans were living in the forests, deserts, plains, mountains, and seashore regions of the vast North American continent. Drawing from the world around them, they created dramatic and colorful designs. They often made pictures of the wild creatures—their "wild brothers"—who shared their world. The images were painted on clay pots and cave walls, or carved on rocks, or engraved on bones, shells, or wood. Some of them were also sculpted in wood and stone, or woven into baskets and blankets. They used them to decorate their homes, canoes, clothes, and even their bodies.

Their materials included clay, wood, reeds, shells, bark, precious stones, wool, and anything else that was available. Their tools were very simple. Shells, rocks, and deer antlers were used to carve images. Paintbrushes were made from twigs, with bristles made of small leaves, hair, or any other soft fiber. Finely ground clay containing minerals was mixed with water to make a red, yellow, or tan color. White paint was made from white earth, and black paint was made by boiling plant juices mixed with charcoal and other ground minerals. Woven baskets and blankets were colored with juice from wild berries and other plants. Other colored dyes were made from minerals that were dug from deep inside the earth.

On the following pages you will see some of these designs. As you study them, think about how you might want to use them. You can either draw them free-hand directly onto a piece of paper, or you can follow the directions on page 9 to copy them exactly. Whichever you choose, it might be fun to create a mural of Indian designs, or to decorate a T-shirt with some, using a permanent felt-tip marker. You might draw a few on a Thanksgiving card. Use the directions on page 18 to make a clay basket and then decorate it with one of the images. There are designs for a fish, frog, turtle, dragonfly, bee, grasshopper, deer, bear, bird, beaver, rabbit, goat, and sheep. There are also some other interesting designs and a sun, moon, and a lightning bolt. Have fun and let your imagination run wild.

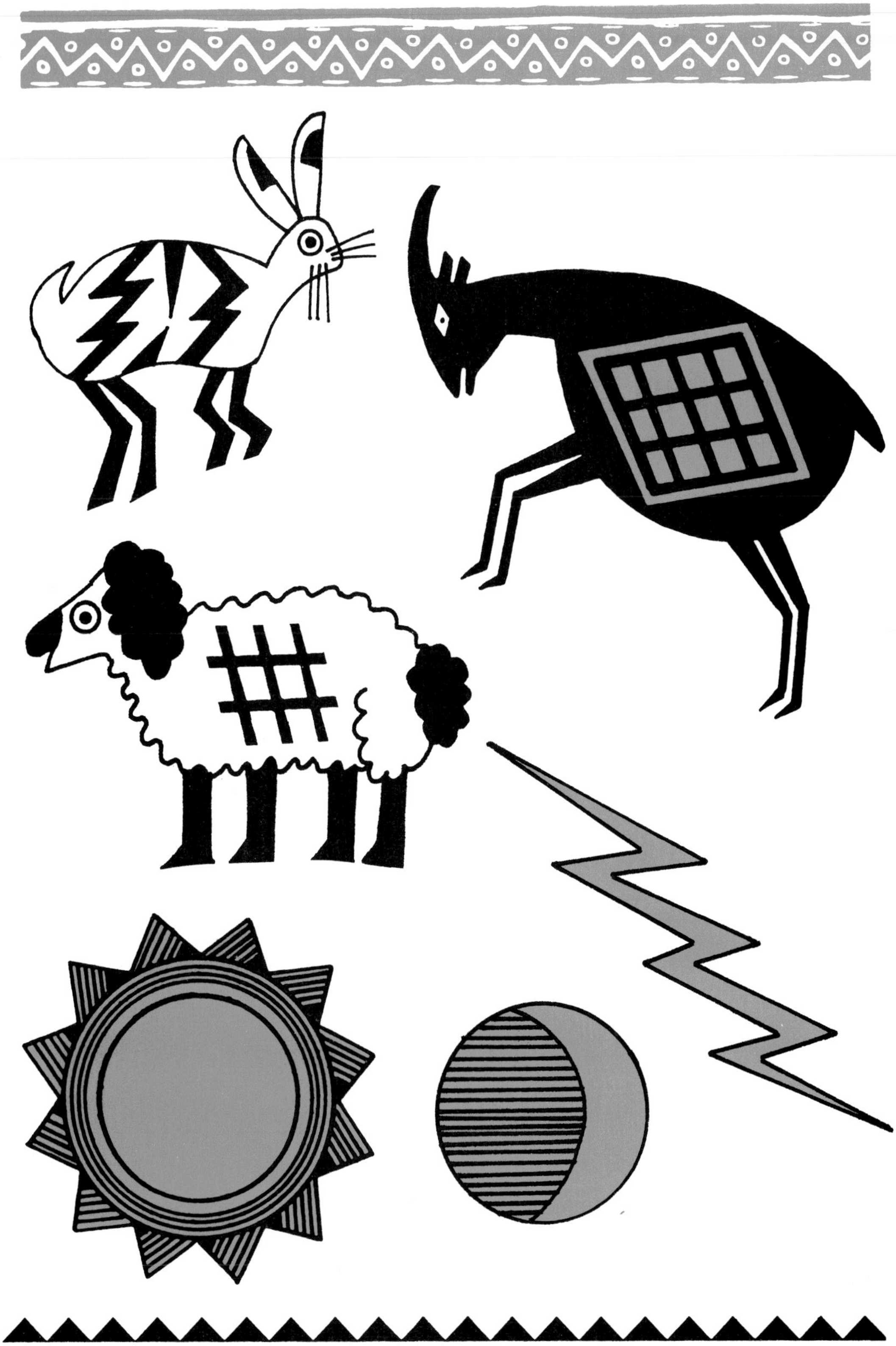

You are invited to share
Thanksgiving dinner
with us, at our house

Pop-Up Turkey Dinner Invitation

Here's a cheerful invitation to dinner that is sure to please everyone who receives it. The turkey pops up from inside the invitation.

HERE'S WHAT YOU WILL NEED★

(These supplies will make 1 invitation)

1 piece of white paper, 8½″ × 11″
5″ square of white oaktag, or other thin cardboard
pencil, tracing paper, scissors
colored pencils, tape

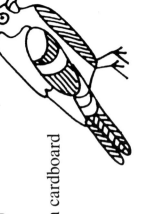

HERE'S HOW TO DO IT★

1. Fold the piece of white paper in half along the 11″ side. Now the folded paper is 8½″ × 5½″. Open it up. This is where you will glue on the turkey later.

2. Take the 5″ square of oaktag and, following the directions given on page 9, trace the turkey design on it. Cut out the turkey.

3. Using colored pencils, color in the turkey's eyes, wings, and tail feathers. Color both sides of the oaktag turkey. Now tape the turkey into the inside fold of the white paper, as shown in the illustration.

4. On the outside write, "You are invited to share Thanksgiving dinner with us, at our house." Add the time, date, and your address. You might also write a Thanksgiving poem on the invitation, like the one on page 10, or create one by yourself.★

Thanksgiving Clay

Here's a simple recipe for a homemade clay that is fun to shape into many things to use in Thanksgiving celebrations, or almost anytime. This is the basic recipe—specific directions for several projects follow.

INGREDIENTS★

1 cup all-purpose flour
½ cup salt
about ⅓ cup water

UTENSILS★

large mixing bowl
mixing fork
measuring cups
plastic bag to store clay in the refrigerator
aluminum foil, cookie sheet, pot holders
pancake turner
felt-tip markers in various colors, pencil, clear nail polish
6" square of cardboard, 12" piece of string
toothpicks to make holes in the clay
a sharp stick, or ballpoint pen to carve into the clay
butter knife to cut the clay
rolling pin

HERE'S HOW TO DO IT★

1. In a large mixing bowl combine the flour and the salt. Gradually add the water. Squeeze the dough with your hands until it is smooth. If the clay gets crumbly, wet your hands with a little water. If the clay gets too wet, sprinkle it with a little more flour and squeeze again. Store the clay in a plastic bag until you are ready to use it.

2. Cover a cookie sheet with aluminum foil. This will be your work surface. Do all your modeling and drying on the sheet. Directions for working with the clay are given in each project description.

3. Finished objects can be dried in the air, or more quickly in the oven. To air-dry your objects, place them on the foil-covered cookie

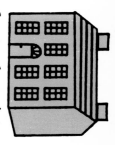

sheet in the sun for a few hours, or let them dry overnight. This way of drying is good for small objects.

4. To oven-dry your objects, place them in the oven. **Ask an adult to help you turn on the oven and set it at low, 225°F.** Bake small, thin objects for about 15 minutes on each side. Bake thick objects for about a half hour on each side.

5. After your objects have dried and cooled, they are ready to be painted with felt-tip markers. To protect the finish on your objects, brush them with two coats of clear nail polish after the colors are dry. This helps to keep the colors from coming off. ★

Thomas Turkey Centerpiece

Thomas Turkey will make a handsome addition to your holiday table. Follow the directions on page 18 to 19 to make the clay. Checking the illustration below, start with a handful of clay and begin to shape it into a turkey. This handful will be the body. From the remaining clay, pinch off a small ball for the head. Attach the head by gently pushing it into the body, and work on shaping it, as shown. Now take more clay to make two wings and a tail feather and attach them. After you are happy with the shape, follow the baking directions and then paint the turkey as you like.

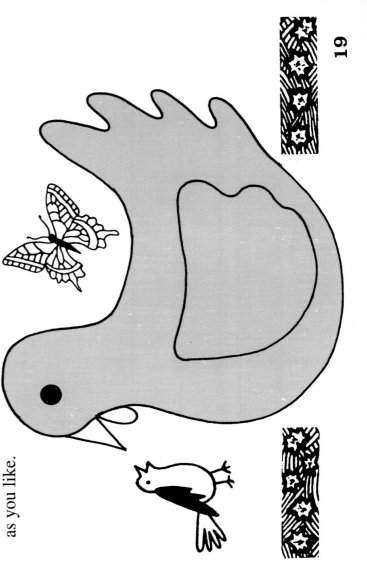

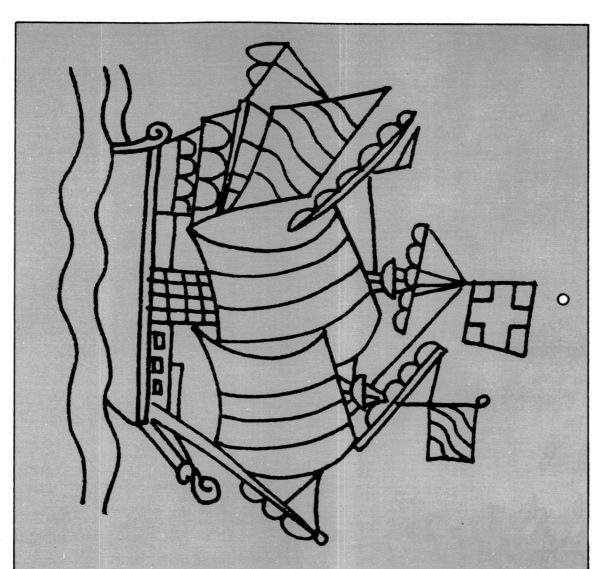

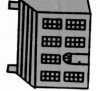

Mayflower Thanksgiving Tile

The *Mayflower*, a cargo ship, carried 102 men, women, and children on a 3,000-mile voyage that took a little over a month. The ship brought them to Plymouth, a place named for the English seaport from which they had set sail. The ship was about 20 years old, and was considered a speedy ship for the time. It could hold 180 tons of cargo. It was probably about 90 feet long from bow to stern and about 25 feet across, at its widest point. Besides food, clothing, a few family treasures, and some small pieces of furniture, the Pilgrims took along a supply of seeds, garden tools, saws, axes, hammers, gunpowder, and firearms. They also brought along barrels of brightly colored beads, cloth, knives, and small mirrors to trade with the Native Americans.

The *Mayflower* set anchor in the port of Plymouth. This was important as it meant the Pilgrims were able to live on board while they built shelters. The ship was a safe place and helped the colonists survive the first long, hard winter.

In the autumn of 1621, the people of Plymouth felt they had good reasons to celebrate. Less than a year before, they had landed on these barren, frozen shores, far from their native England. Now the Pilgrims who survived that first year gave thanks for their chance at a new life in a new land. Their crops had been gathered in and they were thankful that they had been able to grow enough food for the long winter ahead.

HERE'S HOW TO DO IT★

1. Follow the directions given on pages 18–19 for how to make the clay. With a rolling pin, roll out the clay until it is about ¼" thick. Place the 6" square of cardboard on top of the clay. Cut around the edges with the butter knife.

2. Now draw the pattern for the *Mayflower* onto the piece of tracing paper, following the directions given on page 9. Place this pattern on the clay. Pressing hard with the point of a pencil, draw over the lines on the pattern. Lift the pattern off and then go over all of the lines with the pencil. Make sure that the lines are deep enough so that the design will still stand out after the tile has been baked.

3. To hang your tile, make two holes at about ½" from the top, as shown in the illustration. Later, after the tile has been baked and colored, you can push a 12" piece of string through the holes and tie it as shown.

4. Bake the tile in the oven, following the directions given on page 19. Paint the ship's hull brown, the sails white, the ocean blue, and the background yellow. With a black permanent marker, go over the lines for the ropes. Coat the tile with clear nail polish. ★

Miniature Harvest Pots

You can make simply shaped harvest pots, or bowls, using the homemade clay. Follow the directions on pages 18 and 19 for the clay. Then, starting with a handful of clay, make a ball and begin to gently push your thumbs into the center, turning the ball as you work. Checking the illustrations, continue to push the center outward, pinching and shaping it until it looks like a pot. When you have a shape that you are pleased with, dry or bake it. Try decorating it with some of the Native American designs on pages 12 to 15, or with a turkey or pumpkin.

Silhouette Pictures

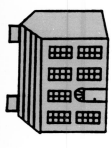

Thanksgiving is a family celebration, so here's a chance to make some old-fashioned portraits of yourself, your friends, and family—and even the family pets, if you can get them to sit still long enough. Silhouette pictures were very popular about 200 years ago, before cameras were invented.

HERE'S WHAT YOU WILL NEED★

paper, tape
black felt-tip marker
a chair and a lamp

HERE'S HOW TO DO IT★

1. Tape the paper to a window. A carefully opened large paper bag works well, or a large sheet of white paper (11″ × 14″). Do not tape it to the wall, as tape leaves marks on walls.

2. Put a chair about two feet in front of the paper. Now put the lamp a foot behind the chair. Turn on the light.

3. Have the person whose portrait is going to be made sit sideways in the chair. Now draw the outline of your subject's shadow on the paper with the black marker. Color in the whole face, as shown in the illustration. Practice exaggerating the person's features, such as the eyelashes, chin, hairstyle, collar, or hair bow. This helps to make the portrait interesting. Look at the examples on this page for ideas. After you have finished making someone's portrait, they can try one of you.★

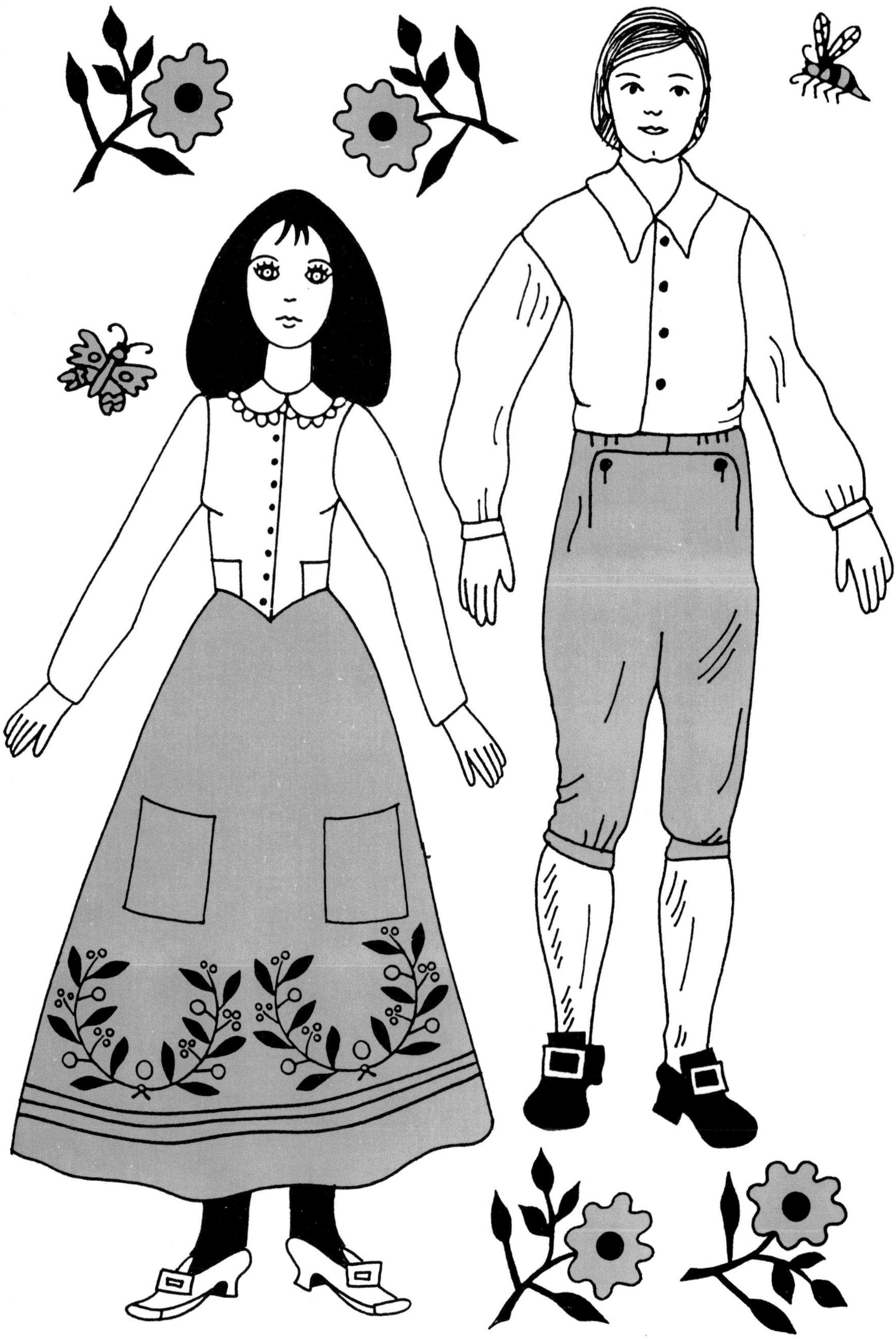

Damaris and Miles

Damaris and Miles were popular names in the 1600s. We will make stand-up figures of Pilgrims that will show what their clothes were like. You might choose other Pilgrim names to use: Faith, Hope, Charity, Elizabeth, or Constance for figures of girls; and Jasper, John, Adam, or William, for boys. Or perhaps you'd like to use two names given to boys who were born on the *Mayflower*. These are Oceanus and Peregrine. Peregrine means pilgrim.

Pilgrim men and boys wore black suits with white collars and cuffs. Their tall black hats had broad brims and silver buckles for decoration. Their dress-up shoes also had buckles. On weekdays they wore gray, brown, or blue linen shirts and woolen or leather breeches, or shorts. Their knit stockings came all the way up their legs. When it was chilly, the men wore sleeveless leather jackets with cloaks over them, instead of coats. They wore a woolen cap called a Monmouth cap in cold weather. The lining of the cloak, or cape, was sometimes a bright color, such as purple. Their clothes were not as drab as we usually imagine.

Women's and girls' clothes were quite lively. Their dresses could be red, purple, bright blue, or green, and had full skirts that reached their ankles. Under a laced bodice they wore a "stomacher" of a different color or material. This was a panel in the front of the dress, almost like a bib. In cold weather, they wore waistcoats or vests, which were usually red. They had cloaks, or capes, like those the men wore, sometimes with hoods. These were usually black, gray, brown, or dark green. Boys wore dresses, which were called coats, until they were six. Besides this, the children's clothes were exactly like those of the adults.

In the Plymouth Colony, in the first few years, there was no time to grow flax to make linen for new clothes. There were no sheep to furnish wool for other articles of clothing. So, the Pilgrims mended their clothes. One stanza of a Pilgrim song tells how they "clouted," or patched, their clothes. Sometimes they even put a patch on top of a patch, or as they said it, "put a clout upon a clout." Now let's try making our Pilgrim figures.

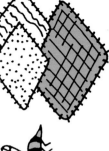

HERE'S WHAT YOU WILL NEED ★

sheet of white oaktag
pencil, tracing paper, scissors
black, fine-line marker
colored pencils or colored markers
cardboard, tape

HERE'S HOW TO DO IT ★

1. Follow the directions on page 9 telling how to trace the patterns from the book. After you have transferred these patterns onto your white oaktag, cut them out.

2. With the black marker, go over all of the pencil lines. Now color in the figures as you like.

3. To make the figures stand up, cut 2 strips of cardboard that are each ½" × 5". Tape one to the back of each figure, as shown in the illustration. Now write the name that you have chosen for each figure on the back as well. Stand the figures up and have fun making up adventures for them. ★

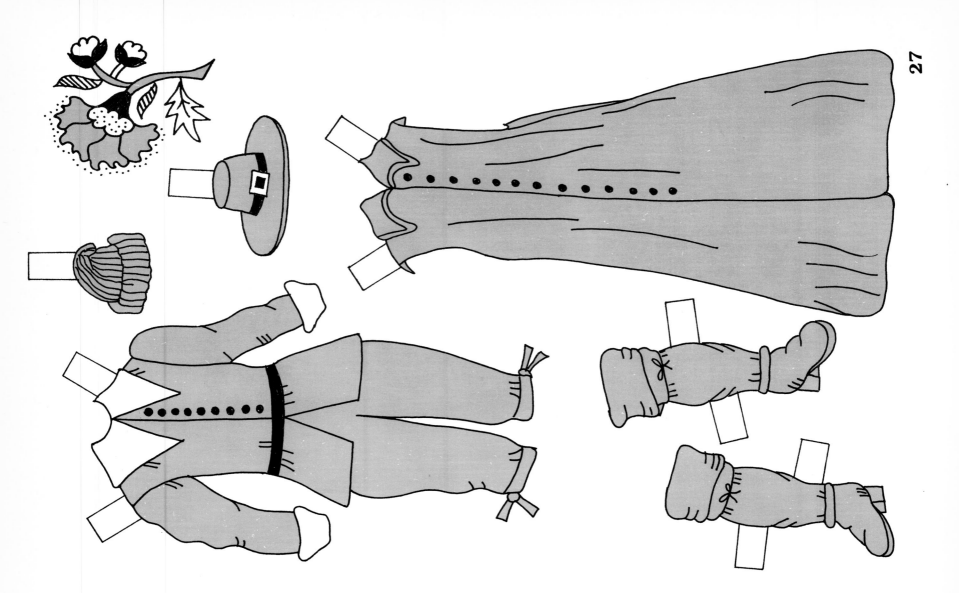

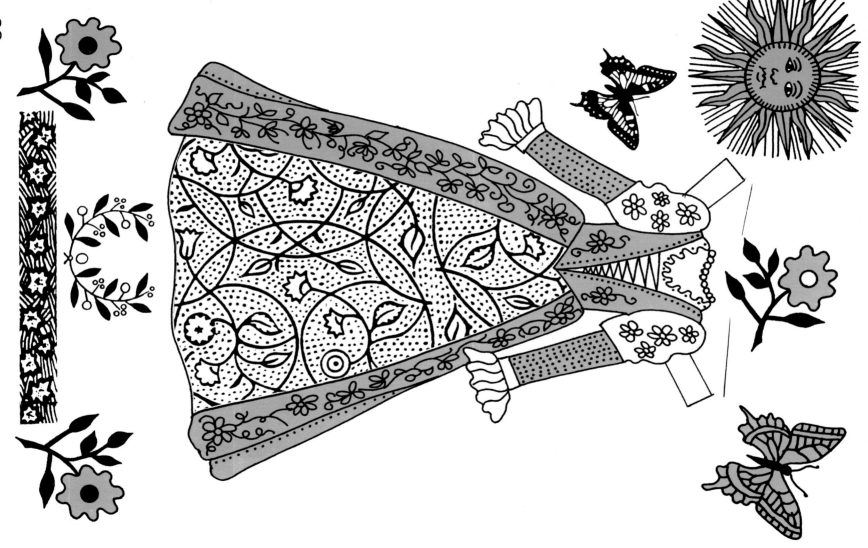

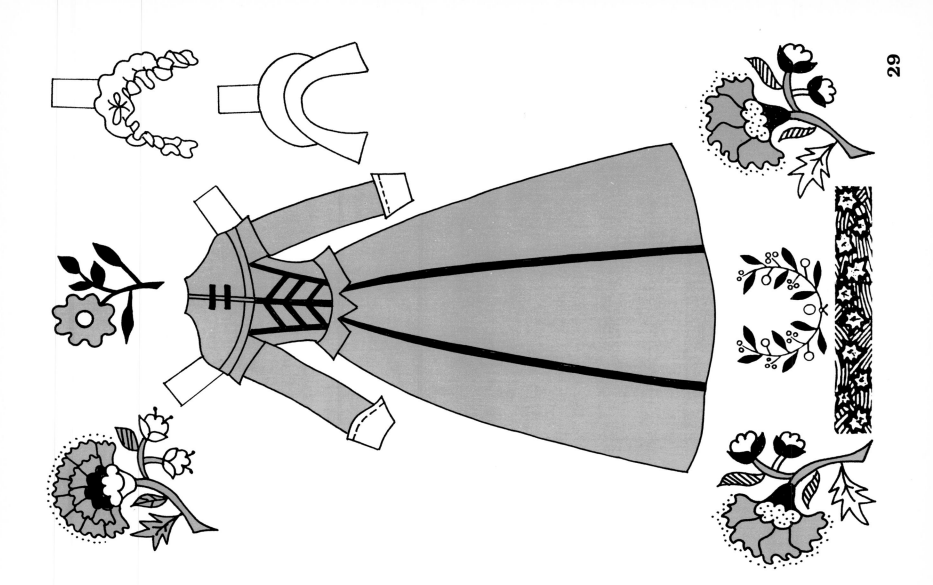

Feathered Friend Feeders

When the days grow shorter and colder, there is less food available for the birds. Birds are a treasured part of our environment. The many different varieties, and their different shapes, colors, and songs add beauty to our surroundings. Many birds are unique to America. Early naturalists, such as Alexander Wilson who lived from 1766 to 1813, walked through the countryside sketching and painting, collecting specimens, taking notes, making observations, and studying bird habits. From his collected information, Wilson wrote *American Ornithology, or The Natural History of the Birds of the United States*. It was engraved and colored from his original drawings, which he made directly from nature. Ornithology is the scientific study of birds. The first volume of his work was published in Philadelphia in the early 1800s. Today some birds have disappeared, but Wilson's work remains and is a valuable record of their existence.

There are four birds here for you to draw. The mockingbird is of special interest because, as noted in Wilson's book, "it was not only peculiar to the new world, but inhabits a very considerable extent of both North and South America; can be traced from the states of New England to Brazil." Thus, the early colonists would have been familiar with it. I've added a hummingbird, robin, and blue jay. Practice drawing them and try making one of the bird feeders, and maybe you will be lucky enough to see these birds. If you grow sunflowers, you can save some of the seeds to feed the birds after the flowers have died.

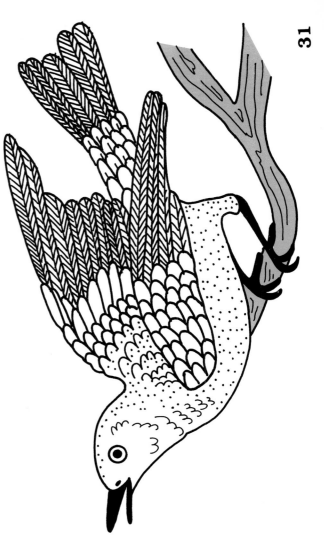

Here are two bird feeders to make. One is made from an orange, the other from a pinecone. Choose which one you would like to try. Your neighborhood birds will certainly appreciate them.

ORANGE BIRD FEEDER★

HERE'S WHAT YOU WILL NEED ★

1 orange (to make 2 bird feeders)
knife
string, 1 piece 48" long, cut into 4 equal pieces
birdseed, dried sunflower seeds, or bread crumbs

HERE'S HOW TO DO IT★

1. Cut the orange in half and carefully pull or scoop out the inside sections. You can eat them or save them for later. Now that you have clean peels, make two holes in each half, as shown in the illustration.

2. Tie a knot at the end of each of the 4 pieces of string. Hang the bird feeders from a tree branch and tie them on, as shown.

3. Fill the bird feeders with birdseed, sunflower seeds, or crumbs. They will last for a few weeks and are sure to please the birds. ★

PINECONE BIRD FEEDER★

HERE'S WHAT YOU WILL NEED★

1 large pinecone
2 tablespoons peanut butter
butter knife
birdseed, in a small bowl
24″ piece of string

HERE'S HOW TO DO IT★

1. Use the butter knife to fill the spaces between the rows of pinecone scales with peanut butter.

2. Roll the pinecone in the birdseed, so that the seeds stick onto the peanut butter.

3. Tie the string around the pinecone, as shown in the illustration. Hang it from a tree branch.★

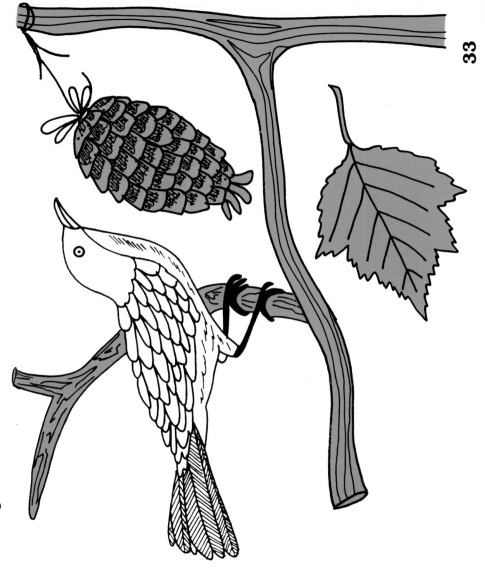

Grow and Harvest a Sunflower

Sunflowers are amazing flowers! Some kinds will grow much taller than you are—6 to 8 feet high. You can grow them in your backyard, a community garden, the school yard, or even on your windowsill. Sunflowers are easy to grow in a sunny place and they shoot up quickly. The flowers are a sunny yellow with a deep brown center. They make terrific centerpieces for a Thanksgiving dinner table, and their seeds can be eaten or shared with the birds.

HERE'S WHAT YOU WILL NEED★

1 packet of sunflower seeds (buy this wherever seeds are sold, in a
  hardware store or in a florist's shop)
garden plot or flowerpots (small, medium, and large size)
small shovel
watering can, strong sticks, rags

HERE'S HOW TO DO IT★

1. Plant your sunflower seeds in the spring, when the ground has gotten a chance to warm up—around the end of April or beginning of May. Scatter a whole packet of seeds over a part of the garden plot and cover them lightly with soil. Water your garden plot, being careful that the seeds are still covered with earth.

2. You must watch your garden as it grows and check that the soil gets enough water. When seedlings appear, pull up some so that the others will have enough room. You can replant the pulled-up seedlings in another spot or in a flowerpot or large empty can.

3. Sunflowers grow quickly and may need support if they are in a windy place. Push a strong stick into the soil near each flower and tie the flower to it with a strip of rag.

4. When the flowers are in full bloom, in the fall, cut some down and make flower arrangements for your table. They will look great.

5. When the flower begins to wither, you can gather the dark, shiny seeds from the center of the flower. Cut off the flower head. Pick the seeds out with your hand.

6. Keep some seeds in a paper bag for planting next year. Dry some in the oven to eat and share with friends. Feed some to the birds in late fall and winter, when their food is scarce. ★

If you want to grow sunflowers on your windowsill, follow the same general directions, except start your seeds in a small yogurt cup or other container. Punch a few drainage holes in the bottom and fill with earth. Put it on a saucer to catch any water that might come through. Push 3 or 4 seeds into the earth and cover them up. Water it whenever the soil seems dry. When the plants begin to grow, they are ready to be moved to 1-pound coffee cans. Ask an adult to make some drainage holes in the bottom of the cans and place a saucer underneath, and gently transplant the seedlings, with their soil, to the cans. Your plants will have to be transferred one final time—into a large plastic container or flowerpot the size of a kitchen garbage can. Again ask an adult to make some drainage holes in the bottom and place a tray or pan underneath it. If you start with 3 or 4 cups, with 4 or 5 seeds in each, you will have plenty of sunflowers. Thin out the plants to 3 or 4 in each container, as they will grow to be very large. Their heads can be 12 inches in diameter and they can stand 6 feet tall. ★

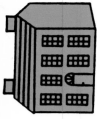

Harvest Pumpkin Bread

While this bread is baking, the kitchen will be full of the old-world smells of the spices of cinnamon, ginger, and cloves that are combined in this wonderful treat. The pumpkin adds moistness to its dark texture.

INGREDIENTS★

½ cup of canned pumpkin
⅔ cup molasses
⅔ cup boiling water
(ask an adult to help you with this)
4 tablespoons sweet butter
1 teaspoon baking soda
1 egg, beaten
1½ cups all-purpose flour
2 teaspoons ground cinnamon
1 teaspoon ground ginger
½ teaspoon ground cloves
extra butter, to grease the pan
confectioners' sugar

UTENSILS★

measuring cups and spoons
large mixing bowl
mixing spoon
9″ square baking pan
pot holders
toothpick
knife, sifter

HERE'S HOW TO DO IT★

1. Ask an adult to help you to turn on the oven. Preheat it to 350°. In the large mixing bowl, blend the pumpkin, sugar, molasses, water, and butter. Allow to cool. Stir in the baking soda, egg, and flour. Stir the mixture well. Now add the cinnamon, ginger, and cloves. Stir until combined. Pour into a greased baking pan.

2. Bake for 30 to 35 minutes or until a toothpick inserted into the center comes out clean. Makes nine 3″ pieces of bread. Sift confectioners' sugar over the cooled bread. ★

Apple Pandowdy

Apples were grown in Europe, in apple orchards, for hundreds of years before America was settled by colonists. The Pilgrims ate apples in England and brought apple seeds and young trees with them to North America. Apple orchards were planted and they grew so well that apples became an American food staple. Wherever colonies were started, apple orchards were planted and enjoyed. Jonathan Chapman of Boston, legend tells us, collected apple seeds from cider mills, dried them, and gave them to people moving west. Later, he also traveled across this wide-open country, planting apple seeds wherever he went. He became known as Johnny Appleseed. Today every state in the country with a temperate climate grows apples. There are hundreds of varieties—some for juice and cider, some for pies, cakes, breads, and sauces, and some just for eating. This is a remarkably useful and delicious fruit.

The original recipe for apple pandowdy came from a handwritten colonial cookbook. It was a common dish, and it was served at breakfast, as a snack, or for dessert.

INGREDIENTS★

1 cup flour
2 teaspoons baking powder
½ teaspoon salt
1 teaspoon cinnamon
1 cup brown sugar, packed
1 cup milk
4 cups apples, peeled and thinly sliced
2 tablespoons butter
extra butter to grease the pan

UTENSILS★

9" square baking pan
mixing bowl and spoon
measuring cups and spoons
pot holders

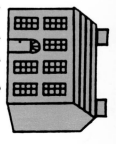

HERE'S HOW TO DO IT★

1. Ask an adult to help you turn on the oven. Preheat the oven to 350°.

2. In the large mixing bowl combine the flour, baking powder, salt, cinnamon, and brown sugar. Add the milk and stir until smooth.

3. Grease a 9" square baking pan. Arrange the sliced apples on the bottom. Pour the batter over the apples. Cut up the 2 tablespoons of butter and arrange over the batter. Bake for about an hour, or until the top is golden brown and springs back when lightly touched. For an extra treat you can serve this with vanilla ice cream. It tastes delicious warm as well as cold. Serves 8.★

Native American Strawberry Corn Bread

Native Americans have several Thanksgiving celebrations. This recipe is taken from their Strawberry Thanksgiving Festival. It is a special festival in which people give thanks for the earth's bounty—in this case the strawberry—and also try to forgive others who have done something wrong to them during the course of the year. Native Americans believe that the beautiful red strawberry is a special gift to share with each other. Let's make this bread and share it with family and friends, or even make an extra loaf to bring to school to share with classmates.

INGREDIENTS★

1 cup cornmeal
1 egg
1 cup all-purpose flour
¼ cup milk
4 teaspoons baking powder
1 pint thawed frozen strawberries
½ teaspoon salt
⅛ cup corn oil
extra oil to grease the baking dish

UTENSILS★

large mixing bowl
mixing spoon
measuring cups and spoons
8″ square baking dish
pot holders

HERE'S HOW TO DO IT★

1. Ask an adult to help you turn on the oven. Preheat the oven to 375°. Grease the baking pan with oil.

2. In the large mixing bowl, stir together the cornmeal, egg, flour, milk, and baking powder. Now add the strawberries, salt, and corn oil. Stir until completely combined. Pour into the baking dish. Bake for 20 to 25 minutes, or until golden brown on top. Cut the cooled bread into 4 rows across, and then cut four rows down, so that you will have 16 pieces. ★

Cranberry-Applesauce Bread

When the Pilgrims landed in North America they were introduced to many new foods by Native Americans. Corn—or maize—popcorn, turkeys, and cranberries, to name just a few. Wild cranberries grew all over the swampy areas near the coast, as far south as today's Virginia. Native Americans used them for food, medicine, and to make a beautiful dye. They preserved them by pounding them into small cakes and then drying them in the sun. Later they used them in soups and stews. Cranberries are a good source of vitamin C. The Pilgrims mixed them with sugar to make sauces, and added them to batters for bread. No one is sure if they were eaten at that first Thanksgiving meal in 1621, but it is certain that they were enjoyed at later ones in the New England colonies. Cranberries are harvested in the fall, around Thanksgiving time, and they are a nice addition to the feast.

This delicious bread combines the apple and the cranberry—one fruit from the Pilgrims' original home country, England, and one from their new home in the colonies of North America.

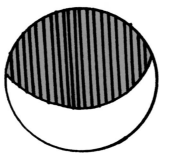

INGREDIENTS★

2 cups all-purpose flour

¾ cup sugar

2 teaspoons baking powder

½ teaspoon baking soda

½ teaspoon salt

1 teaspoon cinnamon

1 cup chunky-style applesauce

½ cup vegetable oil

1 teaspoon vanilla

½ cup cranberries, washed, and with bruised berries discarded

extra oil to grease the pan

UTENSILS★

large mixing bowl

mixing spoon

measuring cups and spoons

9″ × 5″ loaf pan, greased

pot holders, toothpick

HERE'S HOW TO DO IT★

1. Ask an adult to help you turn on the oven. Preheat the oven to 350°.

2. In the large mixing bowl, combine all the ingredients except the cranberries. Work until completely blended. Now carefully add the cranberries and stir until combined.

3. Grease the loaf pan and pour in the batter. Place it in the oven for about an hour. The top should be golden brown and come up an inch or so above the pan. Poke a toothpick into the center of the bread, and if it comes out clean the bread is done.★

Old-fashioned Sugar Cookies

These sugar cookies were my mother's favorite and have become part of our family's tradition. They are great fun to make and shape into turkeys, stars, trees, leaves, hearts, moons, and cats, following the designs on these pages. And the sweet little creatures you make can be shared with family, friends, and neighbors. Or it would be nice to bring a box of them to someone who is needy.

INGREDIENTS★

1 cup butter, softened
1 cup sugar
2 eggs
2 teaspoons vanilla
1/2 teaspoon baking soda
1 teaspoon baking powder
1/2 teaspoon salt
1 teaspoon cinnamon
3 to 3 1/2 cups all-purpose flour
extra flour for rolling out the cookies

UTENSILS★

measuring cups and spoons
large mixing bowl
mixing spoon
plastic wrap
rolling pin
knife, oaktag
pancake turner
cookie sheets covered with aluminum foil
pot holders

HERE'S HOW TO DO IT★

1. In the large mixing bowl, beat the butter until it is creamy. Beat in the sugar, eggs, and vanilla. Stir in the baking soda, baking powder, salt, cinnamon, and 3 cups of flour and mix thoroughly. The dough should be smooth but not too stiff or too sticky. If it doesn't seem right,

44

stir in a little more flour (up to ½ cup). Cover the bowl with plastic wrap and put it in the refrigerator overnight.

2. Spread some extra flour on a clean kitchen counter. Put the dough on it and, with the rolling pin, roll it out to ⅛" thickness. Follow the directions on page 9 and make patterns for your favorite shapes out of oaktag. Place the patterns on the rolled-out dough and cut around them with a knife. Pat the scraps into a ball, roll it out, and make more shapes. Gently, with a pancake turner, lift the cookies onto the cookie sheets.

3. **Ask an adult to help you to turn on the oven and preheat it to 350°.** Bake the cookies for 5 to 7 minutes, or until lightly browned. Makes about 4 dozen cookies. ★

Corn Scones

Scones are little bread cakes that were originally made in England. When the Pilgrims came to North America they adapted their recipes to use the foods that were available here, and so cornmeal was added to ingredients used to make scones. These are even more delicious when served with butter and strawberry jam.

INGREDIENTS★

3/4 cup yellow cornmeal
1 1/2 cups all-purpose flour
1/4 cup firmly packed brown sugar
2 teaspoons baking powder
1/4 teaspoon salt
1/3 cup sweet butter, softened
1/2 cup orange juice
1 egg
1 teaspoon vanilla
extra flour to shape the dough

UTENSILS★

large mixing bowl
mixing spoon
measuring cups and spoons
knife, pot holder
cookie sheet lined with
  aluminum foil

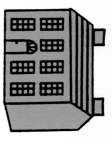

HERE'S HOW TO DO IT★

1. Ask an adult to help you turn on the oven. Preheat the oven to 375°.

2. In the large mixing bowl, stir together the cornmeal, flour, brown sugar, baking powder, and salt. Add the butter and begin to blend it into the mixture. It will look like coarse crumbs. Now add the orange juice, egg, and vanilla. Stir until the batter is completely blended.

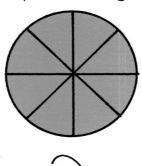

3. Spread some extra flour on a clean kitchen counter and also put some on your hands. Take the dough and form it into a ball. Flatten it, and then shape it into an 8" circle. Place this on the cookie sheet. Use the knife to cut the circle into 8 slices, as shown in the illustration. Bake for 15 to 20 minutes, or until the top is lightly browned on top.★

Thankful for Chocolate Fudge

This velvety, rich chocolate fudge will quickly disappear from your Thanksgiving table.

INGREDIENTS★

½ cup sweet butter
4 cups sugar
1 can (12 ounces) evaporated milk
1 package (12 ounces) semisweet chocolate pieces
1 jar (7 ounces) marshmallow cream
3 teaspoons vanilla
extra butter to grease the pan

UTENSILS★

4-quart saucepan
measuring cups and spoons
mixing spoon
glass of ice water
13″ × 9″ baking pan
knife
aluminum foil

HERE'S HOW TO DO IT★

1. Ask an adult to help you use the stove. In the saucepan, combine the butter, sugar, and evaporated milk. Over medium-high heat cook the mixture, stirring it constantly, until it comes to a full boil. This should take about 10 to 15 minutes. Now turn down the heat and continue stirring the mixture for another 5 minutes. To test that the mixture is properly cooked, drop a small amount (about a ¼ teaspoon) into the glass of ice water. It should form a soft thread. When this test works, remove the pan from the heat.

2. Now add the chocolate pieces. Stir until they are completely melted. Add the marshmallow cream and vanilla, stirring until completely blended.

3. Grease the pan and spread the fudge over the bottom. Cool at room temperature and cut into 1″ squares. You should have 13 rows down the length of your pan and 9 rows across, to make 117 pieces of fudge. Wrap the fudge in aluminum foil and store it in the refrigerator.★

Index

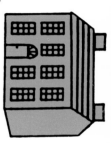